Rockport School
Speech Day 1998
this book is presented to:
F.S.L. Darnley
for:
Geography

Industry

DEBORAH ELLIOTT

Wayland

Titles in the Into Europe series include:
Energy
Environment
Europe's History
Farming
Holidays and Holidaymakers
Industry
Life in Europe
Transport

Picture Acknowledgements
Benetton 41; Chapel Studios 4, 19, 21, 37, 40, 44 (top); Eye Ubiquitous 11 (Paul Thompson), 16 (Paul Seheult), 23 (Nick Wiseman), 28 (Frank Leather), 29 (Nick Wiseman), 30, 32, 33 (John Hulme), 39 (David Cumming), 43 (Sefton); Tony Stone Worldwide cover (top, David James), (bottom, Ken Whitmore); Topham Picture Library 25 (top), 26, 35; Wayland Picture Library 13, 17, 28 (top), 36, 44 (left); Zefa contents page, 5, 7, 8, 9, 10, 15, 20 (both), 22, 23 (top), 24, 25 (bottom), 39. All artwork is by Malcolm Walker.

Designed by Malcolm Walker
Cover pictures: top - The lifting gear and large vats inside a steel mill in Germany. bottom - Worker wearing protective clothing in a chemical factory in France.

Text based on *Industry in Europe* in the Europe series published in 1992.

First published in 1994 by Wayland (Publishers) Limited
61 Western Road, Hove, East Sussex BN3 1JD

© Copyright 1994 Wayland (Publishers) Limited

British Library Cataloguing in Publication Data
Elliott, Deborah
  Industry. - (Into Europe Series)
  I. Title II. Series
  338.4

ISBN 0 7502 1046 X

Typeset by Kudos
Printed and bound by G.Canale & C.S.p.A. in Turin, Italy

Contents

What is industry? 4
Making money 12
Industrial revolutions 16
Power and people 21
Tourism 26
Eastern Europe 29
Western Europe 32
Successes and failures 36
What next? 44
Glossary 46
More information 47
Index 48

What is industry?

Industry makes things which can be sold. Almost every single thing you can think of was made by industry, from chocolate bars to racing cars, from iron, steel and coal to this book. The things produced by industry are called products.

▲ *Many industries worked together to make this book. For example, the timber industry made the paper at this saw mill in Sweden.*

◀ *Fruit pickers picked the grapes for this French wine. The grapes were made into wine at the vineyard. Then the bottling industry packaged the wine ready for sale.*

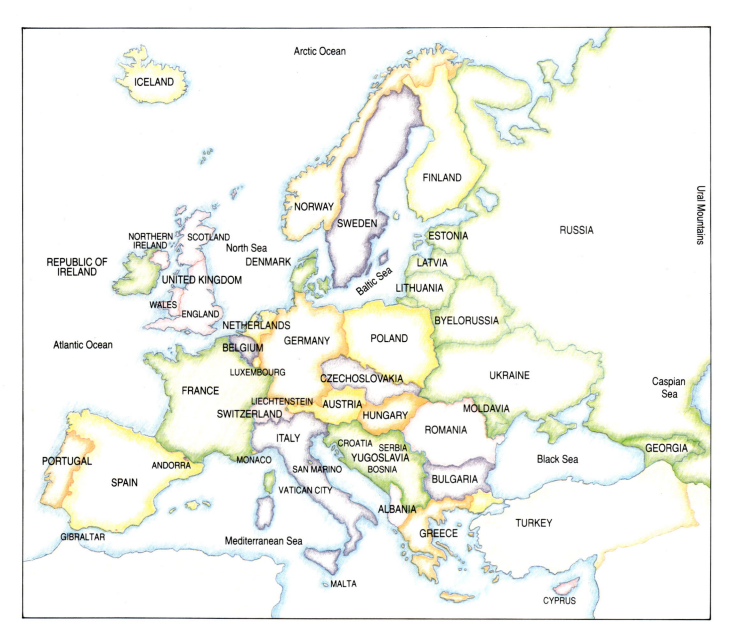

▲ *The paper used to make this book comes from Sweden (see page 5). Ships carried the paper to England where it was made into a book by the publishing industry. The book was printed and bound together in Italy, using machines made in Germany.*

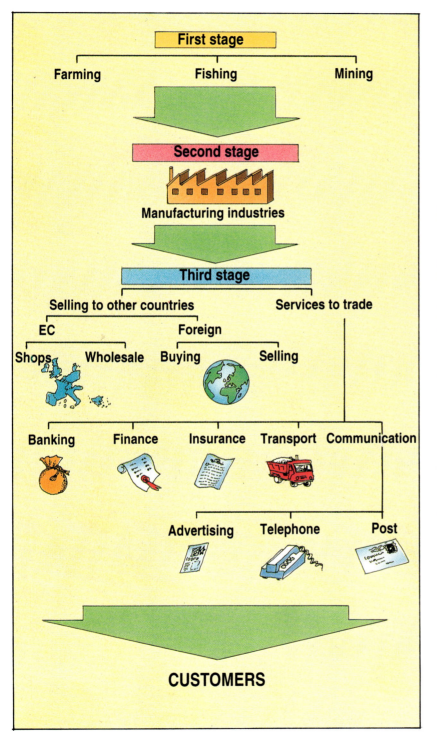

◀ Some of the many industries in Europe.

▼ These industrial businessmen are discussing their day's successes and failures.

▲ Salt being made ready for people to eat, at a factory in Lanzarote.

The percentage of people in Europe who work in farming. ▶

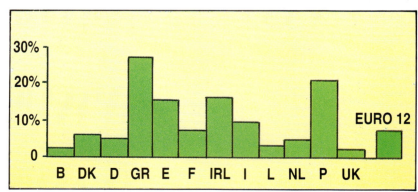

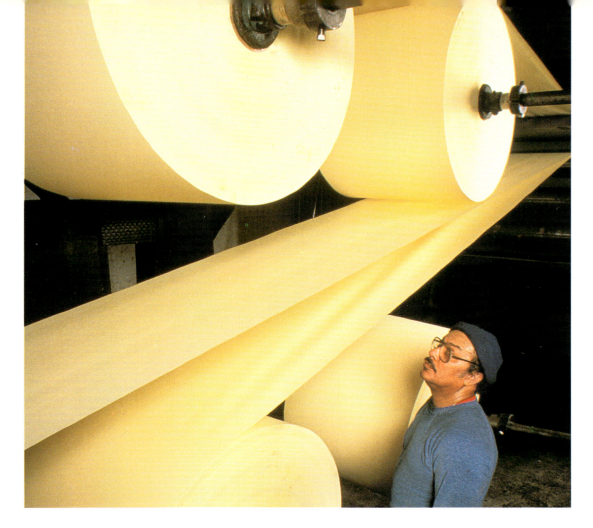

▲ Making sheets of paper for use in this book.

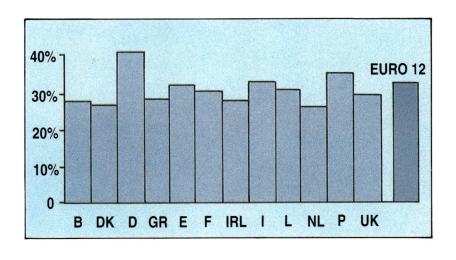

◄ The percentage of people in Europe who work in manufacturing industries. These industries make products from raw materials. For example, making paper from timber.

Some industries are huge, employing thousands of people and making millions of pounds. Other can be very small - managed by one person.

▼ *This flower-seller in Brussels, Belgium has a one-person industry.*

▲ Farming is the most important industry in Portugal. Many people depend on farming for their livelihoods.

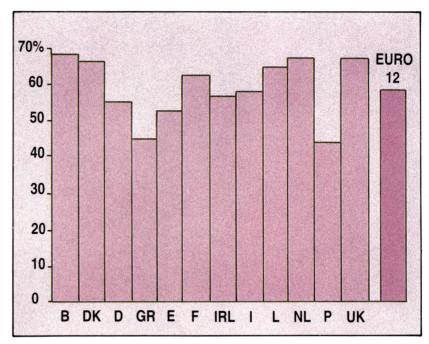

▲ The percentage of people in Europe who work in service industries. These industries include banking, teaching, television and medicine.

The importance of the three types of industry to countries in the European Community (EC) (see page 44). ▶

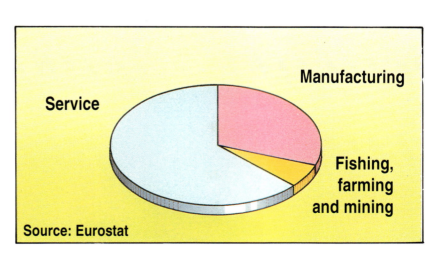

11

Making money

The wealth of a country often depends on the success of that country's industry.

The charts below and opposite show the wealth of different parts of the world and the number of people who live there.

Canada, the USA and Europe have fewer people than most other parts of the world. However, their successful manufacturing industries have made them the wealthiest countries.

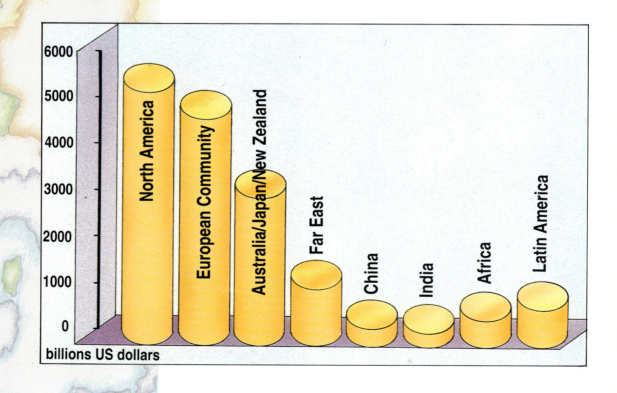

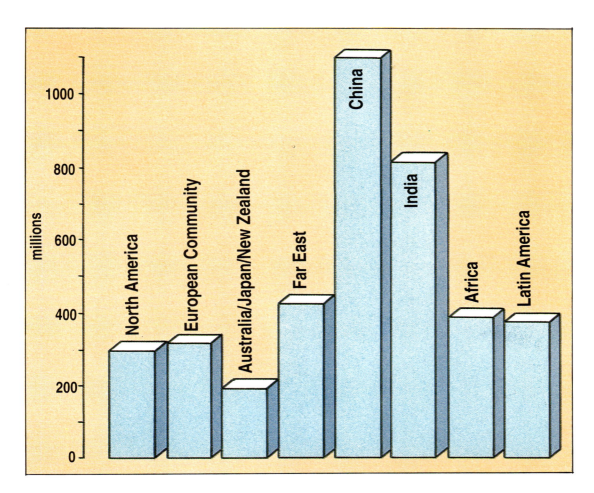

This is a plan of some houses which will be built in Manchester, England.

Most people in Europe can afford to live reasonably well thanks to the success of their countries' industries. ▶

How the wealth is divided up among the countries of Europe. Can you see that Germany has over one-third of the wealth? ▶

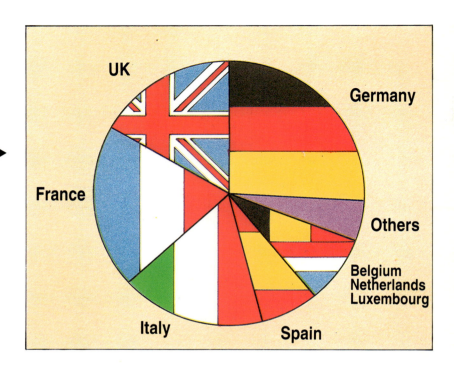

▼ *This chart shows the importance of certain industries in Europe.*

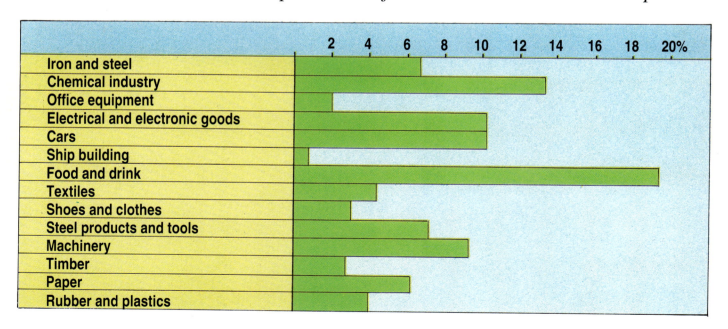

▲ Welding steel panels on to the bottom of a ship. Ship building was one of the most important industries in Britain in the 1800s, when ships were the only form of transport across seas. Now, there are many forms of transport and ship building has become less important.

Industrial revolutions

There have been a number of industrial revolutions in Europe's history. These have been the times when industry has undergone major changes in the way industries work and with the invention of new machines.

The first 'Industrial Revolution' began in Britain in the 1780s. Before that time farming had been the major industry.

Machines were invented which could make more products very quickly. Many people left farming to find jobs in the hundreds of factories being built all over the country.

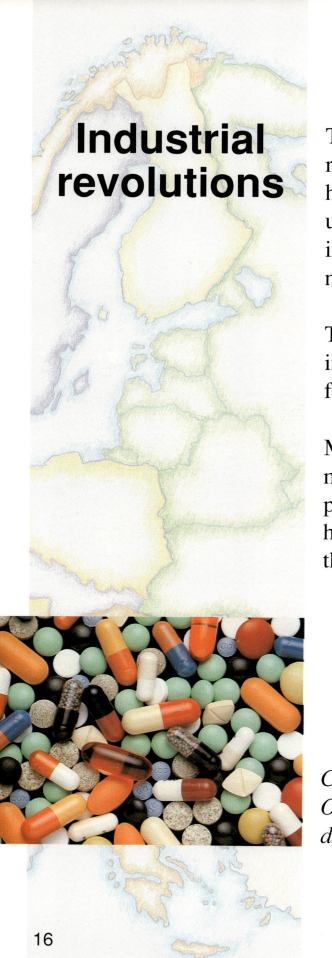

Conditions in the factories were hard. Often, young children were employed to do heavy work for little money. ▶

◀ *Many factory workers were forced to work very long hours with no holidays for very little pay. They wanted to make conditions better, so they formed groups, called unions, which set out certain rights for workers.*

Germany underwent an industrial revolution in the early 1900s. The Ruhr is a region in the west part of Germany. It has the country's largest coalfields. Iron and steel factories were built there because they needed lots of coal.

By 1930, Germany was producing more steel than Britain, and more chemicals than any other country in the world.

Industry was revolutionized yet again with the introduction of production lines. These were lines of people or machines which had to put different pieces of equipment together to make one product.

Production lines meant that goods could be made very quickly and easily. This is called mass production.

The invention of computers caused another major industrial revolution. One computer could do the work of a number of different machines.

▼ *Workers in an electronics factory in France. The different pieces of equipment look very complicated. There is quite a difference between conditions in this factory and the one on page 17.*

◀ At this Mercedes car factory in Germany, a machine is doing a job that was once done by a person.

Most industries today use computers. In fact, the computer industry has become one of the most successful industries.

People all over the world can share information by linking up their computers. This makes industry easier to manage, because people can get information at the touch of a button. ▶

Power and people

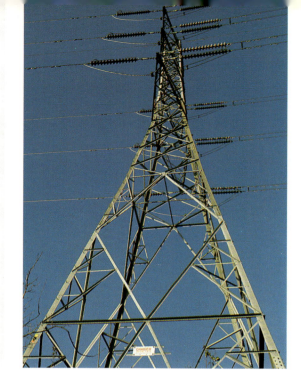

▲ *Pylons dotted across Europe carry electricity from power stations to factories.*

It is clear how much we need industry to make products and money. But what exactly does industry need to work?

Industry needs people to do the jobs, money to buy machines and rent factories and offices, and power to make the machines work.

Most factories in Europe are powered by coal, oil, gas or nuclear energy.

Often factories are built in areas where power is easily available. It is also important that the factories have good transport links, so materials can be brought to the factories and the products can be carried away.

◀ *Rotterdam is a huge and important port in the Netherlands. It lies at the mouth of the Rhine and Mass Rivers. The Rhine flows through Switzerland and Germany.*

Products can be brought by ship to Rotterdam from all over the world, then transported along the Rhine and Mass to the rest of Europe.

◀ *Industry in West Germany grew very quickly in the 1960s. In fact, there were not enough Germans to do all the jobs. So, workers from other European countries, such as Turkey and Yugoslavia, went to work there.*

Factories are often built in areas with lots of people, so there is a definite workforce. In the 1800s and early 1900s, however, factories were built in places with few people. Towns then grew up around the factories, as people moved in search of work. Shops, schools, houses and hospitals were built for the workers.

Industries need the advertising industry to make people know about their products. ▶

Italy

Italy has two quite different parts - the north and the south. Farming is the main industry in the south, which is also much poorer than the north. Many kinds of fruit and vegetables are grown, and farmers also grow tobacco and keep sheep and goats.

The main industries in the north of Italy (above) include making cars, steel, machinery, chemicals and fashion design. In the past few years, the government of Italy has given money to industries to set up in the south of the country.

Industries need good road and rail links to transport their products. ▶

Industries need efficient communication links to work. There are two types of communication link. The first is transport. Industry needs transport to move goods from one place or country to another.

The second communication link is information. As well as goods, industries have to move information. For example, prices or times of delivery of goods often have to be passed from head office to the customer. Telephones, computers and fax machines are the most widely used information links.

◀ *Satellite dishes such as these allow information to be passed quickly from one country to another.*

Tourism

Most industries need other industries to work properly. The tourist industry is a good example of how lots of industries rely on each other and help each other.

◀ All the countries in Europe have a tourist industry. Goods arrive daily from all over the world to be sent to restaurants, hotels and shops for the holidaymakers.

About 100 million people visit Europe each year, making the tourist industry one of the most important. In fact, tourism is the most important industry in Mediterranean countries such as Portugal, Spain, Italy and Greece.

Holidaymakers come to Europe in search of sun, sea, sand, culture and historical buildings. All the countries of Europe have something different to offer.

Italy is one of the most popular countries among holidaymakers. Every year, hundreds of thousands of people visit cities like Florence and Rome. They buy goods made locally, such as leather and pottery, which helps those industries.

The governments in countries of eastern Europe are working hard to encourage tourism. They hope that the tourists will spend lots of money and, as a result, give a boost to other industries.

◀ Boats line up along the quay in the port of Aegina in Greece. The boats are used to show tourists the beautiful Greek coastline and islands.

Over 9 million people visit Greece each year, which, considering the population of Greece is 10 million, shows the importance of tourism.

Tourists from all over the world come to Europe bringing in money to lots of different industries. ▶

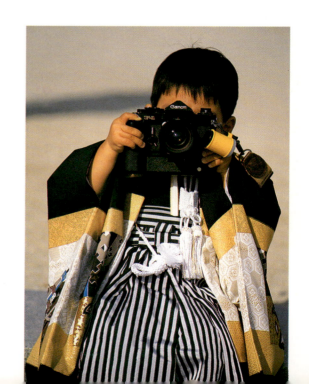

Eastern Europe

Before 1989, the political systems in most eastern European countries meant that industry was controlled by the governments in those countries. Foreign industries were not encouraged to set up businesses. However, there have been tremendous political changes which have affected industry. Now, industries from all over the world are competing to set up in the countries of eastern Europe.

◀ *McDonald's was one of the first fast-food chains to set up in eastern Europe. This store in Moscow in Russia has been a huge hit with the local people.*

◀ *Before 1989, transport links in Russia were poor. This meant that often supplies of food did not reach the shops in time. Now things are beginning to improve.*

Because the countries of eastern Europe avoided contact with influences and ideas from other countries, they did not keep up with changes in industry. New machines and technology made industry in western Europe more efficient. Countries in the west also worked to stop industry harming the environment.

Poland, Czechoslovakia and Hungary are among the countries in the east who are trying to solve the problems faced by their industries. They all suffer from the effects of pollution from industry. The governments are taking advice from industries in the west.

Poland

The political system in Poland changed in 1989. Before, like many countries in eastern Europe, the government in Poland controlled all industry in the country. Most of the industry was inefficient and shops usually had very few goods to sell.

Since 1989, the Polish government has tried to follow the example of industry in western Europe. However, its attempts have not been very successful. Polish people are now paid even less, yet food prices have gone up. Unlike before, there are plenty of western European goods on sale in the shops. But few Poles can afford to buy them.

Poland is also one of the countries most affected by pollution from industry. Before 1989, there were no rules about pollution and the environment. Now, industries are being encouraged to pay special attention to the environment.

◀ *Many industries in what used to be East Germany are trying to catch up with the more modern industries in the west. However, some of the factories in the east are old and run down. They are being closed down and many workers are losing their jobs. There is now a serious problem of unemployment.*

Western Europe

Germany's industries are the third most important in the world, after those in Japan and the USA. Some of the most well-known German industries are making cars (Volkswagen and Mercedes are two famous German car industries), chemicals, and electrical goods. German televisions, videos and computers are sold all over Europe and the rest of the world.

◀ *This advertisement for a German Volkswagen Golf car is in Spain. The German car industry is highly regarded and its cars are driven by many Europeans.*

Spain

Tourism is the most important service industry in this pretty Mediterranean country. Over 45 million holidaymakers visit the resorts along Spain's southern coast every year. The industry provides jobs for over 1 million Spanish people.

In the north of Spain, in the area called the Basque, engineering and ship building are important industries. There are coalfields too, in the city of Bilbao.

Farming is a major industry in the south of Spain. Farmers grow fruit and vegetables for sale in Spain and the rest of Europe.

> Britain was one of the first countries to have coal and iron industries. These are called heavy industries. Because there was such a plentiful supply of the two resources, Britain was able to develop steel and ship building industries in the eighteenth and nineteenth centuries.
>
> Now other European countries, such as France and Germany, have excellent coal industries. In fact, these countries can produce coal so cheaply that even industries in Britain buy coal from them. The coal industry in Britain suffered as a result and many of the coal mines closed down.

France has many industries, including iron, steel, coal, chemicals and cars. French cars are among the most popular in the world. Can you think of any? Peugeot and Renault are the best known.

When many people think of French industry, they immediately think of fashion, design and wine. People all over the world drink wine made from the famous French grapes. French fashion houses make clothes which sell for high prices in high streets in most countries.

Portugal is not known for its industry. It is one of the poorest countries in Europe, despite having a thriving tourist trade. Farming is the country's biggest industry.

◀ *Portugese fishermen set off for the morning's catch.*

Along the coast of Portugal, fishing is one way that people can earn a living. The delicious fish and other kinds of sea food caught along the Portugese shores are sold to local hotels and restaurants, and sent to countries all over Europe.

Successes and failures

▲ *During the 1980s, the building, or construction industry was one of the most successful in Germany, France and Britain. People in those countries clamoured for new and more houses and offices. Building companies made fortunes, which many went on to lose in the early 1990s when a recession hit most European industries.*

A recession is a time when a country's economy is in decline. Industry plays a large part in the successes and failures of a country's economy. If industry works well, and a lot of goods are sold to other countries, then the economy will thrive.

The electronics industry managed to succeed during the recession. People continued to buy videos, televisions and computers, for example. All businesses need electronic equipment.

▼ *How many different pieces of electronic equipment can you see in this office?*

This diagram shows those countries in Europe and the rest of the world with the largest steel industries. ▶

Steel: The main producers	
(figures in millions of tonnes)	1991
Belgium	10.9
France	19.3
Italy	25.1
Netherlands	5.7
Spain	12.7
UK	18.8
Germany	41.1
European Community	138.6
Turkey	7.7
Europe outside EC	25.1
Japan	107.9
USA	88.4
Brazil	25.0
South Korea	21.9
Canada	15.4
India	14.4
South Africa	9.5
Taiwan	8.6
Mexico	7.7
Australia	6.7
WORLD TOTAL*	480.4
*includes other producers	

Steel making was essential to industry in Europe in the first half of this century. Steel was used in ship building and car making. However, since the end of the 1960s Japan, Brazil and Taiwan, among others, have produced steel much more cheaply than the countries of Europe.

◀ Many European steel works closed down during the 1970s and 1980s, and thousands of workers lost their jobs. The steel industry is now beginning to pick up again.

This steel works in Barcelona is the largest of its kind in Spain.

France, Germany, Italy and Britain all have major car industries. However, Japanese companies such as Nissan and Toyota now make and sell their cars in Europe, providing stiff competition to the European companies.

The car in the picture being fitted with an engine is an Aston Martin, made by the British company of the same name. ▶

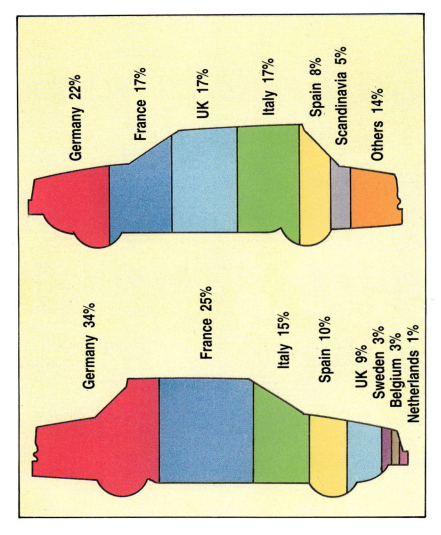

The top diagram on the left shows where in western Europe cars were sold in 1991.

The second diagram shows how many cars were made in the countries of western Europe in the same year.

This is a Trabant, the most popular make of car in former East Germany. Volkswagen, the famous German car company, has bought the company, and now plans to change its design to make it more appealing to all Europeans. ▶

◀ *This is one of the advertisements used by Benetton. The Italian clothing company is infamous for its advertisements. In the past, it has used images of a new-born baby and someone dying from AIDS to advertise its clothes.*

One of the most successful European companies is the Italian clothing company, Benetton. The clothes come in a mixture of bright, vivid colours and are a hit with young people all over the world.

One of the reasons for the company's success is its use of information technology (IT). The cash registers in all the Benetton shops are linked by computer to factories in Italy. This means that people in the factories know immediately what has been sold, which styles are popular and which need to be replaced.

The chemical industry stands out as one of Europe's major success stories. Eight of the ten top world chemical companies are European. Germany has four companies, Britain, France and Italy have one each, and a British-Dutch company has one.

Most industries need chemicals such as plastics, pharmaceuticals (drugs), paints and fertilizers, to work. Because it is so important, the chemical industry has managed to carry on successfully, unlike the iron, steel and coal industries.

▲ Although the European chemical industry is very successful, it can be harmful to the environment. Poisonous fumes are pumped out of factories and power stations.

Most companies have taken measures to control the pollution, although environmental disasters still happen.

What next?

▲ As new machines and technology appear, industry in Europe is changing all the time.

◀ Hopefully there will always be a place for small, one-person industries in Europe.

The countries of the Economic Community (EC), an organization of some European countries which share ideas about industry, farming and energy, for example. ▶

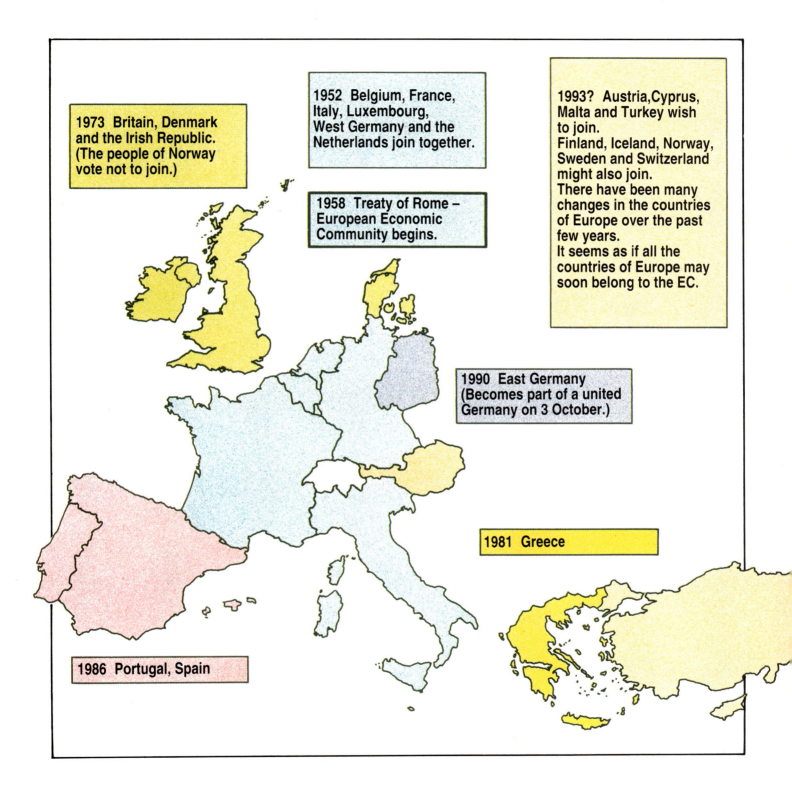

Glossary

communications Ways of passing on imformation from one business or person to another.

design A plan or pattern of how something looks.

economy The money owned by a country which is looked after by the country's government.

efficient Works very well. Something which is inefficient does not work very well.

environment The world around us. For example, animals, plants, rivers, mountains and the air we breathe.

livelihood A person's means of earning a living, such as the money made from his or her job.

percentage The number out of every 100. For example, 10 per cent means 10 out of every 100.

power stations Places where electricity is made.

recession A time when the business affairs of a country are bad and when many people do not have a job.

technology The use of science in industry.

workforce All the people who work for a company, or all the people who are able to work.

More information

Books to read

Food and Farming by John Becklake and Sue Becklake (Franklin Watts, 1991)
Inside France by Ian James (Franklin Watts, 1988)
Inside the Netherlands by Ian James (Franklin Watts, 1990)
Modern Farming by Jeff Battersby (Franklin Watts, 1990)
Our Country series (Wayland, 1991-2)
People and Places series (Macmillan, 1989)

Useful addresses

If you would like more information on industry in Europe, you can write to these organizations.

Chemical Industries Association
Publications Department
Kings Buildings
Smith Square
London SW1P 3JJ

Commission of the European Communities
8 Storey's Gate
London SW1P 3AT

Council of Europe
Boite Postale 431 R6
67006 Strasbourg Cedex
France

Friends of the Earth
26-28 Underwood Street
London N1 7JQ

Index

advertising 23, 41

Britain 15, 16, 34, 36, 39
building (construction) 36

cars 20, 24, 32, 34, 38, 40
chemicals 18, 32, 33, 34, 42-3
coal 4, 18, 34
computers (information technology) 20, 25, 41
cotton 33

eastern Europe 24-31
electronics 19, 37

factories, conditions in 16-18
farming 8, 11, 24, 33, 35

fashion 24, 34
fishing 35
France 5, 34, 36, 39

Germany 6, 14, 18, 20, 23, 32, 36, 39
Greece 27, 28

industrial revolutions 16-20
iron 4, 18, 34
Italy 6, 24, 27, 39, 41

mass production 19

the Netherlands 22

Poland 30, 31
pollution 31, 43
Portugal 11, 27, 35
production lines 19

recession 37

ship building 15, 34, 38
steel 4, 18, 24, 33, 34, 38, 39

timber 5, 9
tourism 26-8
transporting goods 22, 25, 30

unions 18

western Europe 32-5
wine 5, 34